A History of Place

poems by

Mala Hoffman

Finishing Line Press
Georgetown, Kentucky

A History of Place

For Marc

Copyright © 2022 by Mala Hoffman
ISBN 978-1-64662-742-4 First Edition
All rights reserved under International and Pan-American Copyright Conventions. No part of this book may be reproduced in any manner whatsoever without written permission from the publisher, except in the case of brief quotations embodied in critical articles and reviews.

Publisher: Leah Huete de Maines
Editor: Christen Kincaid
Cover Art: Mala Hoffman
Author Photo: Stephanie DePoala
Cover Design: Elizabeth Maines McCleavy

Order online: www.finishinglinepress.com
also available on amazon.com

Author inquiries and mail orders:
Finishing Line Press
PO Box 1626
Georgetown, Kentucky 40324
USA

Table of Contents

Enkenbach 1

Bryant Crescent 2

Somewhere on the Grand Concourse 3

7 Gedney Terrace 5

Motel de Founex 7

Mies 9

Champs D'Aniers, Geneva 10

Amsterdam via Huizen 11

Lord Kitchener Road 13

Beethoven Park 15

Rue de Rochechouart 17

Young Adult Medley 18

Old Mamaroneck Road 23

Pleasantville 25

Almost There 26

Welcome Home 27

Enkenbach

At ten
I return to my first home
Nestled in
a West German village
near enough to the Wiesbaden
hospital of my birth.
I imagine my mother
alone and inexperienced
washing cloth diapers
in cold basins
singing 1940's show tunes
off-key
waiting for my
serviceman father
to return.
Even during that
pilgrimage
a decade later
she was still displaced
a daytime widow
of bank notes
and Ponzi schemes,
soon to be ejected again
out of
false security.

Bryant Crescent

Swinging on a chain
falling onto concrete
emergency room lights
and the smell of disinfectant.
I never forgave that doctor
as he stitched the wound.

How much will Henry
recall
of the fall
we shared
I wonder
as I wince
at the memory.

Somewhere on the Grand Concourse

An apartment
in a building
owned by my uncle
under one of many
more acceptable names,
like Robert or Peter,
than his own—
Abraham.
Two recollections.
Riding on a bus
alone to somewhere
my mother growing smaller
in the window
just beyond my eyes.
The funeral.
John-John's salute
on a tiny square
of black and white
and people sobbing
as the future
is shot
into the past.

7 Gedney Terrace

The house is
a story
onto itself.
A tradesman
maligned for fraud
begs my grandfather
for the job.
He, gentle lion, agrees.
That stable stone raised my father
and later, me
before the European rambling.
I chose yellow paint
for my bedroom,
loved the white-bench breakfast nook
window onto
the neighbor's driveway,
down the road from my friend
Donna's home
where, after a game of cards,
I first learned
that it is different
to be a Jew.

Motel de Founex

Three months—
a trampoline
and Alastair MacLean.
Airport hot dogs
stuck in hollowed out
baguettes,
90-minute drive
to a school
attended for a week,
relief after velvet walls
and casinos
in Divonne.
A moment
of family adventure
when we still recognized
where we came from.

Mies

Trying to shield you
on 300-year-old stone,
steep slopes
worn by Swiss aristocrats
escaping to country houses.
My back
becomes yours
again and still.
Not burdened
by the truth,
you deceive yourself
with hubris
and carelessness.
The debts mount
as one of yours
slips away.

Champ D'Aniers, Geneva

The bus stops
in front of the
apartment complex.
An accordion caterpillar
I ride on my own.
The amphitheater
of the school
reflects nations' acceptance
yet that
never translated
to our band
of American renegades.
We sneak through
fences to "The Bird,"
light cigarettes
and sit on each other's laps
with little regard
for British politesse.
I left before
removal
but only
just.

Amsterdam via Huizen

On my way from train to
bowling alley
each weekend
drinking Amstel
and eating bitterballen with mustard,
a man swathed
in orange
intercepts me.
I must hear the latest
word of God
he says
through the scent
of incense.
I sense
his hypocrisy
and his need
to believe
as he flutters
on the Kalverstraat.
Even now
I wonder
how to find some truth.

Lord Kitchener Road

A grim comedown
from the hopes
of a Paris apartment
this classic Colonial
a dead end
on a dead-end street.
Wings clipped
as car travel
replaces mass transit
and I
at 15
need to walk.
Soon I crawl
out of windows
and into other vehicles,
a poor solution
in a house
with no living room furniture
and a father
in mid-life
flight.

Beethoven Park

The locals called it
"Beeth" hoven,
but it was beautiful nonetheless,
perhaps more so
in our snobby belief
that we were its true appreciators.
College houses
inherited—
The Heartbreak Hotel
The Hedonist—
slouch along curbs
of composer-named streets
contributing only
the clanging of beer bottles
and the arrogance
of transient youth.
After one sunrise in the ER
a 5 a.m. trip
to save a friend
who crashed through a window
trying to fly
we are left
to contemplate
our own complicity
in a community's debris.

Rue de Rochechouart

"Voulez vous courir avec moi?"
he asked
as he ran by
long-limbed
beautiful smile
Clemenceau.
A cute play on words
but I hate running,
still do.
Undeterred
he persisted
with a call to my balcony
Caribbean Romeo
and me
Rapunzel-like still.

I was done with
suitors by then
emotionally burned
as he learned
after a tumble
off his twin bed,
me furiously expunging
an unwanted future

Young Adult Medley

I

A mattress on the floor
labeled contents
in a kitchen
filled with Jesus
and sexual tension.
I stay
for the cocaine
and the job
away from
females woke
before their time.

II

No one warned me,
when signing the lease,
of the laundry habits
on the other side
of the studio door.
Subterranean life
on a pull-out couch
passes to Frances
of butterflies
and "back interest."
The dryer
becomes friendly
company.

III

In the neighborhood
yet not of it
smells of tomato gravy
a magnet for cockroaches.
The kitchen counter
a covered bathtub,
sock-encased keys
gain entry
amid baleful glances
of generational guards.
Even when rescuing
a burning pot.
This could never be home.

IV

Graffiti-infused exile
With George Washington Bridge
views, here I lose
a brother to gain
a spouse,
though not as clear-cut as that.
Let's just say
I held solitude
close
in hopes
of letting it go.

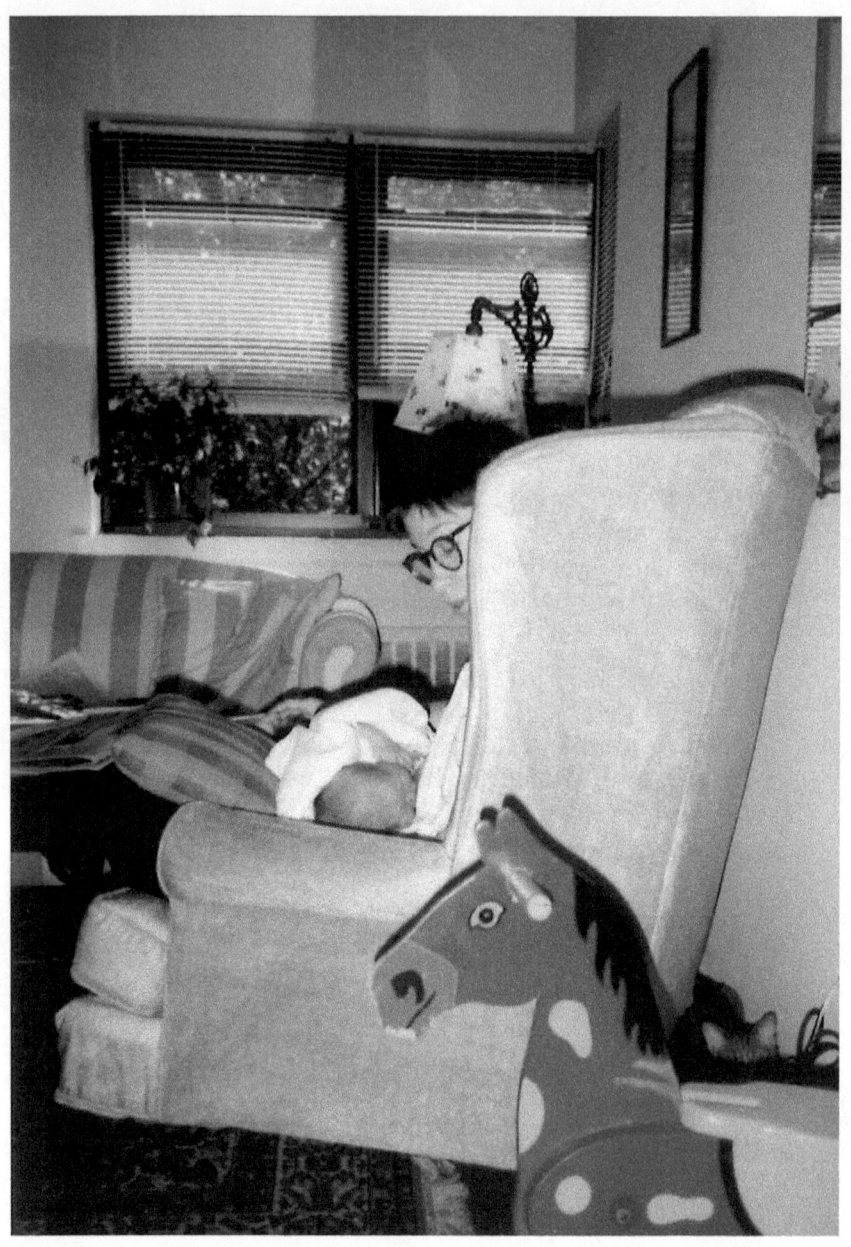

Old Mamaroneck Road

A bittersweet entry
signals a departure.
Memories of raisin cake
and gin rummy
Folger's coffee
prepared by the spoonful.
We clear
to prepare—
beaded purses
Devonshire tea cups
dozens of unopened
decks of cards.
We congratulate ourselves
that this unveiling
is prior to death
though she dies
soon enough
one in a row of wheelchairs
lining a clinical hallway
devoid of her charm.
This space harbors
the next generation
and a cat
named Simone.

Pleasantville

We are literally
on the wrong side
of the tracks,
though it takes
a few months
and a friend's move
to the right side
to realize it.
Still, at five years
it becomes the
longest I've lived
anywhere.
A Sears catalog house
with an asbestos-clad
octopus
as the heater in
the basement,
we live in fear
that the one man
who can service it
will die or retire.
We leave
before he does.
Our daughters' futures
hang
In the imbalance

Almost There

I

Peach trees
and wraparound porch,
a cul-de-sac
with old friends as
neighbors
at the end.
It's a quick drive
to the center
of your hometown.
Soon
A basement playroom
is visited by Santa
during a Christmas
of loss.
We are getting closer.

II

In your childhood room
throat pocked with strep
it's a waiting game
as shale is cracked
foundation laid
the bones of a house
grow into skeletal rooms.
We were here
but not here,
stretching across
imagination
to create our permanent shelter

Welcome Home

It doesn't happen
right away
the warm blanket feeling
the pause
in motion.
Two decades
pass
enough to ignore
specifics
leave retrospectives
and examine the whole.
We built this house
then continued building
daily
monthly
yearly
until we all became
a part of it.
For our daughters,
a childhood home.
For me,
me.

Mala Hoffman is a poet and educator who lives in Gardiner, N.Y. She was born in and spent a number of years growing up in Europe, which inspired this collection. She is also a former journalist who continues to contribute opinion pieces to a variety of publications.

Her poetry has appeared in the *Village Voice, Chronogram, Awosting Alchemy* and *Literary Gazette*, among others. Several of her poems have been accepted into anthologies including *edna, Riverine* and *A Slant of Light*. Her poetry collections include *Half Moon Over Midnight* (Paper Kite Press), *A Year of Wednesdays* (Finishing Line Press) and *Becoming Bubbe* (The Poet's Haven).

www.ingramcontent.com/pod-product-compliance
Lightning Source LLC
LaVergne TN
LVHW041515070426
835507LV00012B/1576